Common Core Math Edition
1st Grade
Workbook Series

Speedy Publishing LLC
40 E. Main St. #1156
Newark, DE 19711
www.speedypublishing.com

Counting Objects (1-20)

Circle 11 fishes.

Counting Objects (1-20)

Circle 13 oranges.

Counting Objects (1-20)

Circle 17 apples.

Counting Objects (1-20)

Circle 10 strawberries.

Counting Objects (1-20)

Circle 14 carrots.

Number Patterns

Fill in the blanks. Count by 3.

3		9		15
18	21		27	
		39	42	
48	51			60
63	66			75

Number Patterns

Fill in the blanks. Count by 5.

5		15		25
30				50
			70	75
80	85			
105				125

Number Patterns

Fill in the blanks. Count by 2.

2		6		10
12				20
22	24			
		36	38	40
42				50

Number Patterns

Fill in the blanks. Count by 4.

4				20
24	28			
		52	56	60
64	68		76	80
84	88			

Addition

Adding two single-digit numbers.

1. 6 + 9 = _____

2. 0 + 9 = _____

3. 4 + 9 = _____

4. 7 + 7 = _____

5. 3 + 6 = _____

6. 4 + 2 = _____

7. 2 + 6 = _____

8. 1 + 9 = _____

9. 0 + 0 = _____

10. 2 + 7 = _____

Addition

Adding two single-digit numbers.

1. 6 + 8 = _____

2. 3 + 8 = _____

3. 3 + 9 = _____

4. 1 + 8 = _____

5. 6 + 4 = _____

6. 2 + 9 = _____

7. 0 + 3 = _____

8. 2 + 4 = _____

9. 3 + 9 = _____

10. 9 + 4 = _____

Addition

Adding two single-digit numbers.

1. 1 + 5 = ____

2. 7 + 3 = ____

3. 7 + 0 = ____

4. 9 + 9 = ____

5. 6 + 6 = ____

6. 6 + 5 = ____

7. 2 + 2 = ____

8. 4 + 0 = ____

9. 9 + 3 = ____

10. 8 + 1 = ____

Addition

Adding two single-digit numbers.

1. 5 + 2 = _____

2. 5 + 9 = _____

3. 9 + 3 = _____

4. 0 + 3 = _____

5. 3 + 9 = _____

6. 1 + 4 = _____

7. 2 + 2 = _____

8. 7 + 0 = _____

9. 7 + 1 = _____

10. 4 + 9 = _____

Addition

Adding two single-digit numbers.

1. 3 + 0 = ____

2. 1 + 6 = ____

3. 3 + 4 = ____

4. 8 + 0 = ____

5. 4 + 4 = ____

6. 5 + 4 = ____

7. 8 + 8 = ____

8. 0 + 5 = ____

9. 2 + 7 = ____

10. 3 + 6 = ____

Addition

Adding two single-digit numbers.

1. 0 + 1 = _____

2. 8 + 7 = _____

3. 1 + 4 = _____

4. 2 + 5 = _____

5. 9 + 1 = _____

6. 3 + 3 = _____

7. 5 + 7 = _____

8. 7 + 1 = _____

9. 8 + 9 = _____

10. 0 + 4 = _____

Subtraction

Subtracting within 10-19.

1. 16 – 6 = _____
2. 19 – 6 = _____
3. 14 – 2 = _____
4. 15 – 4 = _____
5. 17 – 5 = _____

6. 15 – 2 = _____
7. 18 – 6 = _____
8. 16 – 0 = _____
9. 16 – 3 = _____
10. 19 – 2 = _____

Subtraction

Subtracting within 10-19.

1. 17 – 3 = _____   6. 13 – 0 = _____

2. 14 – 3 = _____   7. 17 – 1 = _____

3. 19 – 1 = _____   8. 18 – 4 = _____

4. 15 – 11 = _____   9. 19 – 9 = _____

5. 13 – 2 = _____   10. 14 – 1 = _____

Subtraction

Subtracting within 10-19.

1. $16 - 6 =$ _____

2. $17 - 5 =$ _____

3. $16 - 4 =$ _____

4. $18 - 7 =$ _____

5. $15 - 13 =$ _____

6. $13 - 3 =$ _____

7. $15 - 3 =$ _____

8. $14 - 2 =$ _____

9. $15 - 11 =$ _____

10. $15 - 4 =$ _____

Subtraction

Subtracting within 10-19.

1. 13 – 2 = _______

2. 19 – 7 = _______

3. 19 – 5 = _______

4. 15 – 12 = _______

5. 17 – 6 = _______

6. 17 – 2 = _______

7. 18 – 8 = _______

8. 14 – 4 = _______

9. 16 – 14 = _______

10. 18 – 6 = _______

Subtraction

Subtracting within 10-19.

1. 15 − 3 = _____

2. 18 − 7 = _____

3. 16 − 5 = _____

4. 17 − 3 = _____

5. 18 − 6 = _____

6. 15 − 13 = _____

7. 19 − 3 = _____

8. 17 − 7 = _____

9. 16 − 6 = _____

10. 13 − 11 = _____

Subtraction

Subtracting within 10-19.

1. 15 − 4 = _____   **6.** 12 − 2 = _____

2. 18 − 5 = _____   **7.** 17 − 5 = _____

3. 17 − 1 = _____   **8.** 17 − 6 = _____

4. 13 − 2 = _____   **9.** 16 − 3 = _____

5. 19 − 2 = _____   **10.** 13 − 1 = _____

Place Values

Identifying place values.

	hundreds	tens	ones
42			
17			
64			
19			

Place Values

Identifying place values.

	hundreds	tens	ones
108			
126			
176			
163			

Place Values

Identifying place values.

	hundreds	tens	ones
39			
139			
76			
44			

Place Values

Identifying place values.

	hundreds	tens	ones
189			
96			
32			
7			

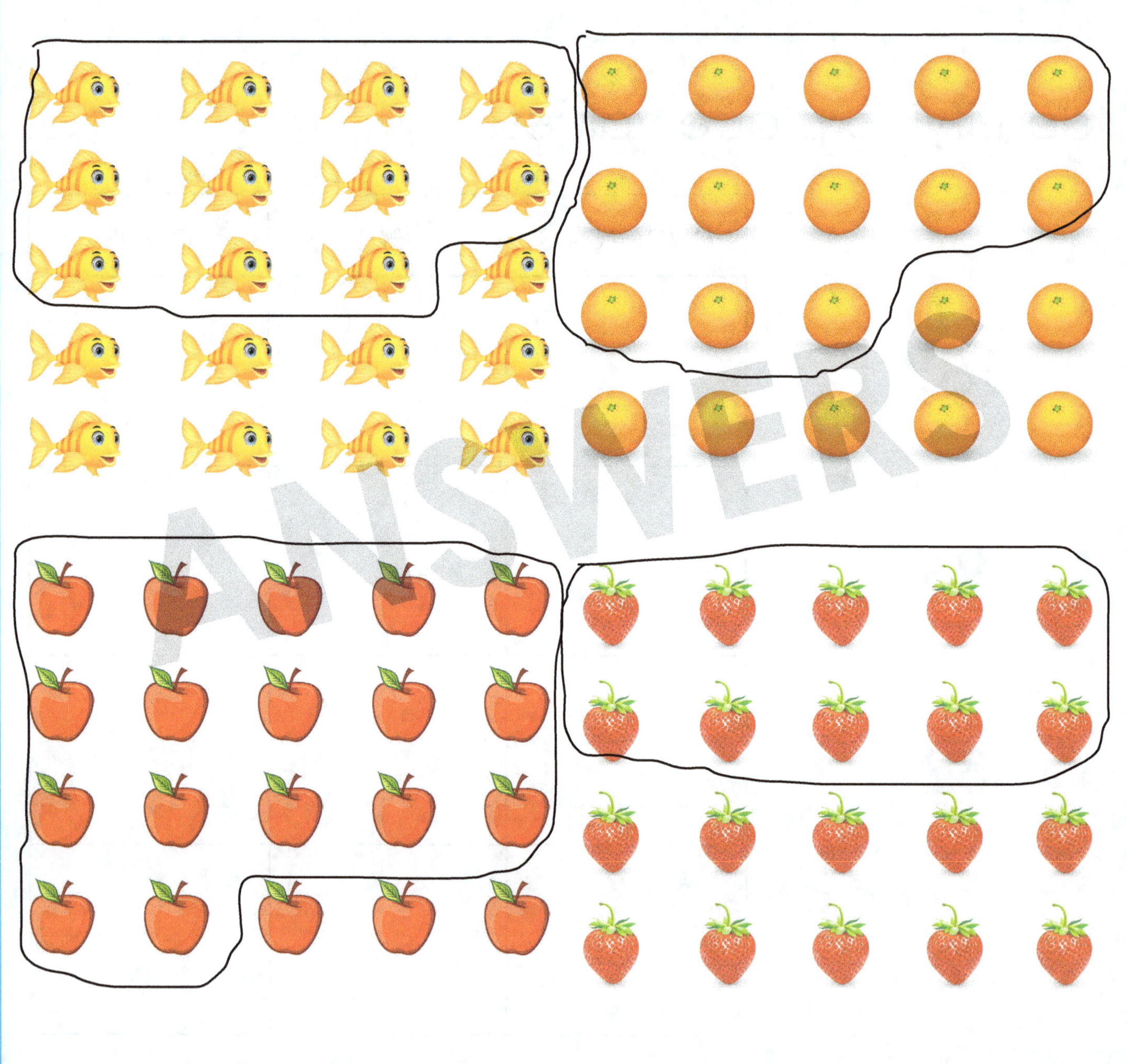

3	6	9	12	15
18	21	24	27	30
33	36	39	42	45
48	51	54	57	60
63	66	69	72	75

2	4	6	8	10
12	14	16	18	20
22	24	26	28	30
32	34	36	38	40
42	44	46	48	50

5	10	15	20	25
30	35	40	45	50
55	60	65	70	75
80	85	90	95	100
105	110	115	120	125

4	8	12	16	20
24	28	32	36	40
44	48	52	56	60
64	68	72	76	80
84	88	92	96	100

#		#		#		#	
1.	15	1.	7	1.	10	1.	11
2.	9	2.	14	2.	13	2.	12
3.	13	3.	12	3.	12	3.	14
4.	14	4.	3	4.	11	4.	3
5.	9	5.	12	5.	12	5.	11
6.	6	6.	5	6.	13	6.	15
7.	8	7.	4	7.	12	7.	10
8.	10	8.	7	8.	16	8.	10
9.	0	9.	8	9.	13	9.	2
10.	9	10.	13	10.	17	10.	12

#		#		#		#	
1.	14	1.	3	1.	14	1.	12
2.	11	2.	7	2.	11	2.	11
3.	12	3.	7	3.	18	3.	11
4.	9	4.	8	4.	4	4.	14
5.	10	5.	8	5.	11	5.	12
6.	11	6.	9	6.	13	6.	2
7.	3	7.	16	7.	16	7.	16
8.	6	8.	5	8.	14	8.	10
9.	12	9.	9	9.	10	9.	10
10.	13	10.	9	10.	13	10.	2

#		#		#		#	
1.	6	1.	1	1.	10	1.	11
2.	10	2.	15	2.	12	2.	13
3.	7	3.	5	3.	12	3.	16
4.	18	4.	7	4.	11	4.	11
5.	12	5.	10	5.	2	5.	17
6.	11	6.	6	6.	10	6.	10
7.	4	7.	12	7.	12	7.	12
8.	4	8.	8	8.	12	8.	11
9.	12	9.	17	9.	4	9.	13
10.	9	10.	4	10.	11	10.	12

	hundreds	tens	ones
42		4	2
17		1	7
64		6	4
19		1	9

	hundreds	tens	ones
108	1	0	8
126	1	2	6
176	1	7	6
163	1	6	3

	hundreds	tens	ones
39		3	9
139	1	3	9
76		7	6
44		4	4

	hundreds	tens	ones
189	1	8	9
96		9	6
32		3	2
7			7